To:

_____

From:

_____

Date:

_____

Message:

_____

_____

_____

Morning
Glories

Jeanette Lockerbie

MOODY
The Name You Can Trust®
A MINISTRY OF MOODY BIBLE INSTITUTE

MORNING GLORIES by Jeanette Lockerbie

© 1999: Christian Art
         PO Box 1599
         Vereeniging
         1930
         South Africa

This book was first published in the United States by Moody Press with
the title of *Morning Glories*, copyright © 1987 by the Moody Bible
Institute of Chicago.

Designed by: Christian Art

ISBN 08024-4753-8

Printed in Singapore.

Everything's coming up new

Bible Reading: Ezekiel 36:24-28

A new heart ... will I give you, and a
new spirit will I put within you (v. 26).

*M*arian sighed as she looked out the window. *Monday morning – and here I am in the same old rut.*

Do you ever feel you're in some kind of rut? Maybe we all do at times, even though we know that this is no part of God's plan for us. God is not the creator of ruts. Rather, He promises us a whole series of new things: new experiences, new paths to travel with Him, all of which have their beginnings with His free offer of a new heart and a new spirit.

A new heart. The cynic of today might argue, "But modern medical skill and knowledge are capable of

6

giving anyone a new heart."

Our reply could be, "Yes. You may be able to get a new heart *if* ...

you are a medically viable candidate
your insurance covers the cost
you are willing to risk the percentages

— and even then there is no guarantee."

We need to keep in mind, also, that there is much more than a "medical cure" inherent in God's offer. This new heart means a total change: "Old things are passed away; behold all things are become new" (2 Corinthians 5:17).

Note, too, that this is a twofold offer: new heart, new spirit. Not even the most dedicated, the most highly skilled and experienced surgeon can implant a new *spirit* in his patient!

Here is another new thing we are promised in God's Word: a new *song* (Psalm 40:3).

You may not be a soloist or even a member of the choir, but one day you will be, if you have this new heart.

I recall a chorus we used to sing:

I have a song in my heart today,
Something I never had.
Jesus has come, and my cup overruns;
Oh, say, but I'm glad.

For the soul-inspiring words of the song we will join in when we reach heaven, see Revelation 5:9-13.

It would take more than this whole little book to talk about all the new things – both in this life and the life to come – that God has in store for the new in heart.

How do we get this new heart?

We have to *want* it. We have to be dissatisfied with having a sin-prone heart – and we have to confess this to God and ask Him to forgive us for Jesus' sake.

Only then will we have a new heart and a new spirit that will put a new song on our lips, and that will make us recipients of God's mercies that are new every morning (Lamentations 3:22-23).

Tapping into our legacy

Bible Reading: John 14:25-29

*Peace I leave with you ... Let not your heart
be troubled, neither let it be afraid (v. 27).*

The Lord Jesus had just talked with His disciples about His imminent departure from them. Well He knew that turbulent days lay ahead of them in a hostile world. To encourage their hearts, and as a bulwark against the evil days, He gave them the promise of a special legacy: *peace*. This was not just any kind of peace – it was His peace, a peace such as the world had never known.

And the wonderful thing about this peace is that you and I, His blood-bought children, are coheirs of this legacy.

I was reminded that this asset is mine as, just a few days ago on a transatlantic flight, the red "Fasten your safety belt" sign blinked on, and the captain issued his warning of turbulence ahead. I immediately tensed with fear, even though I had never encountered a really frightening experience in the air. Then the words came to me, as though spoken by the Lord Himself, "Let not your heart be troubled, neither let it be afraid." How reas-suring it was to realize that those are *His* words, not just those of one neighbor saying to another, "Don't be afraid; there's really nothing to be afraid of." I'm not putting down such well-intentioned words. We should be ready to offer comfort and aid whenever we can. But no matter how sincere we are, we may be quite unable to do anything to alleviate another's fears. The words of Jesus, by contrast, carry with them the power to banish our worst anxieties and replace them with His peace.

Another benefit of this legacy of peace is that it will never be all used up. I know a woman who for many years looked forward to a promised legacy.

Sadly, when the would-be benefactor died, there was barely enough to pay final expenses and attorney's fees. For the Christian there can never be such disappointment. Whatever our need for peace, however often we lay claim to our promised legacy, there will always be an abundant supply.

Another gratifying result of living on this legacy is that it adds solid weight to our credibility as Christians. The non-Christians around us have their own problems; they don't need us adding ours. Oh, we all have problems, and always will in this world. But we know where to take ours, and the resultant tranquillity of spirit we enjoy can speak volumes to those around us for whom we may be praying.

What better way to share an inheritance?

Things go better with thanks

Bible Reading: Ephesians 5:15-20

I will bless the Lord at all times: his
praise shall continually be in my mouth.
Psalm 34:1

Joan and Eileen were commiserating with one another in their aloneness. Joan, a recently widowed young woman, badly needed someone who would really listen to her minutely detailed accounts of her husband's sudden death. Eileen, whose husband had left her for another woman, gently interjected, "And some people are telling me, as they probably tell you, 'Just thank the Lord and keep on going.'" Should you thank God for the death of the one who means everything to you – the awful finality of it, the loss of lover, protector, provider, daily companion, and partner in life's adventures?

Thank God for divorce or desertion – the emotional clobbering, the ego-shattering, the feelings of failure and guilt, in addition to the practical ramifications – thank Him for all of these? Yes, if we would heed what the Bible teaches.

It is Bible truth; nevertheless few Christians, while they are going through a severe trial, want to be told to "just praise the Lord." Nor will a sensitive fellow believer spray around such phrases at such a time.

It takes a powerful measure of spiritual maturity to ride the waves when you lose your husband. Most people flounder, for a while at least, and possibly the last thing they want to hear is platitudes such as "praise the Lord." Even so, things do go better with *thanks*.

There are at least two reasons this is so. First, the Bible bids us: "In everything give thanks; for this is the will of God ... concerning you" (1 Thessalonians 5:18). Second, God has promised to be with us in trouble (Psalm 91:15), so we can thank Him for this. The heart of the matter is that we thank God because, as believers in Him, it is the right thing to do, and obedience is its own reward.

I wouldn't pretend to know *how* praise and thanksgiving work; I just know they do. I tend not to be analytical about the things that work for me; I'm just thankful for them. After all, what difference would it make if we did understand all about what makes things "tick"? Would that make them more effective? If we were restricted in daily life solely to the use and enjoyment of things we wholly understand, what a narrow experience that would be, to say nothing of the advantages we would have to forego. For example, what do we understand about electricity? All I know about it is that it dispels darkness, makes the temperature bearable, and performs innumerable other services – even though I'm totally ignorant of how it works!

In like manner I'm ignorant of how the Spirit operates in my life, but as I learn to trust Him, I'm finding out that everything goes better with thanks.

There are no silly questions

Bible Reading: John 14:5-9, 22-26

Jesus answered him.
John 13:36,38

J am not a compulsive seminar attendee, nevertheless I recognize that some have been valuable to me. In one, the leader prefaced his discussion period with, "Remember, there is no such thing as a silly question."

What a freeing concept, I thought, *and such a practical thing for a mother to keep in mind.*

Questions are here to be handled, whether we like them or not; and who among us has not at times been weary of the eternal why, why, why?

We do have alternatives when someone comes at us with questions. We can turn them off with, "What a silly question!" Or we can just listen (frequently the question itself is a bid for attention, as we all know), or we can give their question our best shot.

It pays not to fudge. If we don't know the answer, there's nothing wrong with an honest, "I don't know the answer to this one, son." The child will appreciate our honesty. And imagine – something Mom doesn't know! Then we can go the next step and learn together. And there's something warm and companionable about two heads over one book. It may be, in days to come when the particular piece of knowledge comes into use for them, your son and daughter will remember that Mother took time to search for it with them.

In addition, the response with which his questions are met at home will shape a child's thinking as to the worth of asking other adults for helpful information. For example, if Mary's mother always turns her off and never makes an attempt to answer her questions, this girl will undoubtedly grow up thinking, *What's the use of asking? They never tell you anything*. And this attitude will include others besides her parents.

I will always be grateful to the seminar speaker who showed me that there are no silly questions.

That makes me ponder how much we are indebted to the disciples and their questions of the Lord Jesus as they walked together. Jesus did not turn from them; nor did He consider their questions silly or trivial. He answered as He alone could, and today in the gospels we can read and be blessed by His answers.

Helping a child cope with change

Bible Reading: Hebrews 13:5

He hath said, I will never leave thee, nor forsake thee (v. 5).

Change can be threatening whatever one's age: for a child it can be traumatic. It's up to the parents, when the change is significant as in a family's relocating, to prepare the child. When such preparation is neglected, it can create problems for the family. I heard recently of such a situation.

Four-year-old Jason's family had just moved to a new town, and on their first Sunday there they sought out a church. Arriving in time for Sunday school, they were greeted, then Jason was whisked off to his new class. On the way home his dad asked, "How do you like your new Sunday school, son?" And to the parents' dismay Jason blurted out, "I hate it; I *hate* it! They put me in a class full of children *all by myself!*"

I laughed at first when I heard it. But I realize there was nothing funny about it to little Jason. It could take quite a few Sundays to erase his first feeling of being abandoned when he found himself "alone" in his classroom.

It's not difficult for me to empathize with this child: I still recall the time when my family moved to a new area. We were not at that time a church-going family, but my mother felt I should attend Sunday school. I was older at that time than little Jason, and I just didn't go the first two weeks my parents sent me (I arrived home on time, and nobody questioned me as to what I had learned or how I had liked my class). I had simply not risked exposing myself to people among whom I would have felt alone.

We need to keep in mind, however, that all children are different. Some are born adventurers: for them, the family move opens up all kinds of possibilities; they can hardly wait to get going, even though they've been happy in their present surroundings.

So we need to consider what is important to the child, to assure him of the things that will *not* change. Yes, he can take his puppy, his favorite toys. He can write and possibly visit the friends he's leaving (at this point he doesn't want to hear about the "nice new kids" he will meet).

Above all, the child must be assured that Jesus will go with him; that He will be there with him in their new home, at school, and that *Jesus never changes.*

Handled with loving concern, a family move can prepare children for later significant changes in their lives. So it's vital that in all the hassle of moving, the child's feelings and fears are recognized.

Whatever our age, we can comfort ourselves with God's unfailing promise *I will never leave you or forsake you.*

Witnessing without pushing

Bible Reading: John 4:1-29

*Come, see a man who told me all things
that ever I did: is not this the Christ? (v. 29).*

Possibly one of the most common excuses given by persons who have heard the gospel but who have never made any kind of commitment to Jesus Christ is, "I had religion pushed down my throat."

Nobody wants to be thought of as being pushy. But are we? Some people undoubtedly are. I was gratified one day recently when I received a review of one of my books. In recommending it, the reviewer had summed up his comments with, "The author is not a pushy Christian. She helps the reader share his faith."

Generally, the intent of the aggressive Christian cannot be questioned; it's his approach that leaves much to be desired. As an insightful Christian stated, "If people gag on our methods, they won't get our message."

Let's look at the opposite tactic: nonaggressive, relaxed, easy sharing in the attempt to introduce someone to Jesus.

Our Lord is Himself the perfect example of how to witness. We cannot fail to observe how He took time and met the person on the basis of his or her interests before confronting the individual with the decisive issue of eternal life. The woman at the well is a case in point.

Think of your own experience (if, like me, you grew up in a nonevangelical situation). You probably have a firm recollection of how you first came to know about Jesus, the Savior. Was it an experience that still warms your heart as you think of how thoughtfully you were dealt with by another Christian? Or do you shake your head as you think it over and say, "It's a wonder I even listened, the way they tried to push salvation down my throat"?

I was in my late teens when I was first brought face-to-face with a personal God, a personal Jesus. It was in the home of non-Christian friends, and that evening another visitor, a young evangelist, was present. While some played table games, a few were listening to the preacher. I edged toward them. He was speaking about what he called "the second coming of Christ," and to me it sounded like pure fantasy – Arabian Nights' stuff. I kept listening and not understanding one little bit. But one thing I did understand: before we broke up, he asked our hostess if he might pray, and, permission granted, he prayed briefly for each one *by name*.

That was the first time I had ever met someone who knew God well enough to talk to Him about *me*. That was my introduction to Christianity on the personal level.

I might never have responded to a pushy Christian. We need to keep in mind, however, that we are all different.

Some people will respond only to an aggressive approach. What may be regarded as overzealousness by one individual will be quite acceptable to another – and vice versa. So we need to be sensitive. We can be quite sure that the Holy Spirit is never pushy – and we have Christ's promise that His Spirit will guide us.

Doing the "to dos"

Bible Reading: Ecclesiastes 3:1-8

To every thing there is a season (v. 1).

There's a great satisfaction in seeing the slate wiped clean of "things to do." In addition, there can sometimes be a special reward. Let me share this instance with you: I had received a letter from a minister friend who explained that, due to heart problems, he was leaving the active pastorate and planned to serve the Lord through writing. He was asking me for some pointers.

Like many others, I tend to let my personal mail pile up "until I have time." I don't know why I answered this particular letter so promptly. But I did, offering some encouragement and practical suggestions. Barely one week had elapsed when I received a letter from this minister's wife. "Thank you so much for your good letter to David," she wrote, and she added, "The Lord took him home last night."

Even as my heart went out to this new widow, I realized that God was speaking to me. How glad I was that I had taken time to reply at once, rather than putting it off, even though the Lord knew this old friend would have no further need of human help.

If this experience would say anything it is this: *do it now*. Just three little words. But what a wealth of advice. So often we leave undone things that could so easily be taken care of if we would but do it now.

What if one of those things is seeking forgiveness from someone we have offended or wronged? We put it off, possibly waiting for the other person to make the first move, or we're waiting for the right time. There is no remorse so keen as that of knowing we have neglected to do something – and now it is too late. The opportunity is gone forever.

What if the Holy Spirit is gently nudging us to go and share the gospel with a shut-in or an unchurched neighbor? Isn't now the time to do it? Not often does God dramatically remind us of the uncertainty of life – that *today is ours*, and tomorrow may be too late. But common sense and practicality echo that this is so.

"No time like the present," we quip to each other. A cliché, I know. Nevertheless it is a worthwhile precept, and putting precept into practice can often be accomplished just by heeding three little words.

How often it is not the actual tasks themselves that tire us out; it's the never-get-done, frustrating image they conjure up in our minds: "I have to do this – and this – and this –" and a mountain of jobs blurs our vision of the two or three we could be doing while we're sighing over those that are waiting to be done. It's somehow easier for us to lament, "There's so much to do," than to get busy and attack things one at a time.

A proven way to help us implement our resolve to do it now is to make this a matter of daily prayer. Tell the Lord your problem. Ask Him to strengthen your determination. God will enable anyone who really wants to, to *do it now.*

When you can't understand

Bible Reading: Ephesians 6:10-15

Put on the whole armour of God ... And having done all, ... stand (vv. 11,13).

*M*y oldest brother is a minister of the gospel. One Sunday morning when I was visiting, he preached on "The Whole Armor of God." Like others in his congregation I had heard sermons on that topic before. But never had I been so impressed with one word in the text: *stand.*

It was not so much the word itself but the preacher's comment on that word that was so unforgettable to me: "Notice that God says 'stand'; He does not say 'understand.'"

Just as explicit as the directions concerning donning the armor – piece by piece – is this injunction to do nothing but stand.

"But, God," you may argue, "surely there's something I can do.

We've heard these verses; many of us have memorized them. But we are people of action. We're not good at standing still. How often I've murmured as I've had to wait for something or somebody, "I've no background for waiting around doing nothing."

If we have to just stand, we want to know at least the why of it.

God does not have to explain to us, His creatures. We can fuss and fume and tap our toes, impatient over not being able to understand. The "stand" command irks us. Yet God does not give commands in order to frustrate us.

Someday we will know all the answers. Meanwhile we can learn the lesson of trusting in the dark.

In some specific instances the Lord has brought my brother's insightful sermon to my mind to pass on to someone who needed such consolation. A surgeon friend, for instance, had taken extraordinary measures to save a young accident victim, even enlisting the willing aid of the U.S. Surgeon General, Dr. C. Everett Koop. But "having done all," our friend saw the boy die and was having a struggle over "Why, God?" For him that early morning the words "Stand, therefore" came like balm from heaven. It will always be so when, having done all, we let God be God and heed His injunction to us to stand even when we cannot understand.

Making the good people nice

Bible Reading: 1 Peter 1:3-8

You rejoice with joy unspeakable (v. 8).

$\mathcal{R}$iding a bus one day, I overheard this statement: "Christians may not have made the world any better, but they surely have made it duller."

We could shrug off this criticism as sheer cynicism. Maybe, however, we can profit by questioning what occasions such a comment.

Then there's the prayer of a five year old, "O God, please make the bad people good and the good people nice."

Something is behind the insightful recognition by a child that "good" and "nice" should go together.

What is "nice" to a five year old? Generally, it's joy and happiness, the good-to-be-with feeling one gives the child. "My teacher's *nice*" is generally accompanied by shining eyes and a warm smile. "Nice" is a good thing, a pleasant thing to be.

Why is good not always pleasant?

David the psalmist knew the two go together. He wrote, "How good and pleasant ..." (Psalm 133:1). *Both* good and pleasant. Not like medicine, which, it is said, the more effective it is, the more unpleasant to the taste. I recall an evil-tasting concoction my mother used to dispense (on principle, I think, rather than prescription). The name of it was Henry's Solution, and as a youngster one of my goals was to get even with this "Henry" – maybe make him drink a quart of his own medicine.

Have you thought that this is how some people regard us and our professed Christianity?

They question, "Does it have to be so unpalatable?"

It may be that they have been disillusioned, that sensing or knowing that Christ promises joy and happiness, they have nevertheless had as models Christians who project an image of gloom. Such persons can't know for themselves all the benefits of being a Christian until they have first tasted and found that the Lord is good (Psalm 34:8). Meanwhile they need good samples, and we who (perhaps all unknowingly) are offering these samples need to demonstrate that our faith in Christ is working for us; our inner Christian joy must show on the outside.

Christian joy doesn't come in a spray can. We can't turn it on and off like an aerosol. It's the deep spring of living water that Jesus promised would bubble up in the hearts of those who believe, and it is both good and pleasant. It need never be grim.

I'll think about it

Bible Reading: Philippians 4:4-8

Finally, brethren ... think on these things (v. 8).

*H*ow often have you asked someone to do something and been met with, "I'll have to think about it"? Thinking is something we all do. It is not confined to the intellectual, the well-educated, the affluent, the people who have lots of time. Everyone is a thinker, and although only God and we ourselves know what our thoughts are, inevitably our actions will reflect our thinking.

But do we consider to what extent our "thinking about it" influences our subsequent actions – what we are and what we do?

Suppose we were making a list of the best things to think about. Where would we start? Wouldn't it be enlightening to jot down the thoughts that have occupied our minds over the last hour? "As [a man] thinks in his heart, so is he" (Proverbs 23:7).

As free agents, we can let our thoughts roam where we will. We can dig around in the soil of our mind, cultivating all kinds of thoughts: complaints, criticism of others, envy, jealousy of another person's possessions, talents, looks, position. Or, we can take a different tack. Consider Paul's "whatevers" –

> truth   honesty   justice
> purity   loveliness   good reputation

– qualities summed up as virtuous and praiseworthy.

But how do we do this? Surrounded as we are with all kinds of people and every conceivable form of input, how can we effectively guard our thoughts?

One proven method is this: when you find a worthless thought invading your mind, recognize it as such, and ask yourself, *Why am I countenancing such a thought?* Then, quickly replace it with something *from the mind of God*: quote a Bible verse, aloud if the situation will allow. (I can't think of a better reason for memorizing Scripture than to have it on tap for such occasions.)

Although a "good thought" of our own might be an antidote to wrong thinking, there are times when it would not be powerful enough. The Word of God is always "quick and powerful" (see Hebrews 4:12) and "is a discerner of the thoughts and intents of the heart." Think of that!

Since it is a fact that each of us is responsible for her thoughts, a daily morning prayer such as David's "let ... the meditation of my heart be acceptable in thy sight" (Psalm 19:14) will do much to arm us against unbidden thoughts. Our good thinking will then be reflected in our actions.

Asking more than God asks

Bible Reading: Ephesians 4:29-32

Be kind and compassionate ... forgiving each other.
v. 32, NIV*

$\mathcal{S}$ome people promote themselves to being God in the lives of others.

Alice's mother was such a person. To be sure, she was motivated by her love for her daughter. Alice's husband, Joe, had been anything but a good husband. Although Alice was not a complainer, her mother knew her daughter was unhappy. Then one day Alice phoned from the distant state she and Joe had moved to. "Mom," she exclaimed, "know what? *Joe accepted the Lord* – and, oh, everything is *so* different!" The phone line couldn't cloud the joy in Alice's voice as she exulted in what was happening in their lives.

But on the other end of the line was no reciprocal joy. In a cynical voice, the mother responded, "I'll believe it when I see it. It'll take more than this phone call to convince me that there's any change in *that* man!"

"Oh, *Mother*," Alice replied, "I thought you would be overjoyed."

A "hm" was the response.

"What *will* it take, Mom, for you to believe Joe – to forgive him?"

"Here's what it will take, Alice. You make Joe sit right down and write me *himself*, confessing all the wrong he's done and all the unhappiness he's brought on you. I want it in his words, not yours. I want to be sure he has really repented and is really a changed man. Maybe then I'll forgive him. But he'll have to prove himself!"

Write a statement of confession and contrition to your in-laws? Isn't that asking more of a penitent than God in heaven does? Nowhere in the Bible do we read, "Thou shalt confess to thy mother-in-law and therefore prove thyself."

But part of the "proof" was that Joe, rather than resenting his mother-in-law's demand, complied with it. Nevertheless she maintained her "wait and see" attitude while asserting how bighearted she was in "forgiving" her son-in-law.

The couple's happy life in the years that followed was

ample evidence that the letter had been written with a true motive, not just to pacify a mother-in-law. Meanwhile she herself lost out on the joy that accompanies a genuinely forgiving spirit.

New International Version

When you run out of a future

Bible Reading: Deuteronomy 32:11; Jeremiah 29:11

*"For I know the plans that I have for you," declares
the Lord ... "to give you a future and a hope".
Jeremiah 29:11, NASB**

$\mathcal{H}$ow can one run out of a future?

When the last child is grown and gone from the home,
some women do feel that they have run out of a future.
You may happen to be one of them.

The wedding is over. The last of the guests has gone,
and you're sitting down to catch your breath after the
many months of happy, hectic preparations.

In a few days the house is back to normal. *Normal?*
you think ruefully. *With my last child gone from the
home! With a great gaping emptiness in my life? Is it*

normal not to have a daughter or son calling downstairs, "Mom, please, I'm in a big hurry, will you do this or that for me?" Is it normal not to have them monopolize the bathroom or the telephone – and fill the house with their happy, noisy, hungry friends?

Frequently the mother sighs and weeps inwardly as she resigns herself to a kind of half-life. How well I remember the day my son rode off with his lovely bride, properly leaving his parents to cleave to the girl he had chosen as his life's mate. And can I ever forget the December day when, through ghostlike fog, a ship sailed out of Vancouver harbor bearing our only daughter half a world away to the mission field? I confess that my spirits that day matched the bleakness of the weather. No, I had not run out of a future, but I did have a gap in my life.

Few of us are so mature as to easily realize that we're not less mothers just because we are not so much needed as we have been – that our family members do not love us less than they always have.

I want to say right here that I don't buy into the concept propagated by some psychologists that a mother "runs out of a future" when she has no one left to *manipulate*.

We could all take a lesson from the biblical story of the mother eagle. She "stirs up her nest," encouraging her young to try out their own wings. Oh, she is there, fluttering around and ready to save them should they appear to fall. But once they have proved that their wings are strong enough to bear them, they are on their own. (And it's nowhere recorded that the mother eagles get together and lament that their nests are empty; it's a natural expectation.)

Whatever our reactions to change, one thing is certain. God deals in futures; His promise is crystal clear.

I know the plans I have for you. They are plans for good and not for evil, to give you a future and a hope.

New American Standard Bible.

How can giving be sinful?

Bible Reading: Matthew 2:9-11

They presented unto him gifts (v. 11).

$\mathcal{M}$arie and Beth had met for lunch in a mall that buzzed with Christmas shoppers. Noticing that her friend was strangely quiet, Beth asked, "Something bothering you, Marie?"

After some hesitation, Marie answered, "It's all *this*," making a sweeping gesture with her hand. "Here I am racking my brains to think of the 'right gift' – and it seems to me that mostly they're for people who already have everything –"

"Me, too," her friend cut in.

"So why are we doing it?"

"Custom," suggested Beth. "We know it's the thing to do. And, besides, what would Christmas be like if we cut out the gift-giving?"

"I know what you're saying, Beth. But this year? With all the hunger and want and misery in our world! Do we have to be trapped into the crass commercialism of our day? Don't we have an alternative?

More and more we're finding individuals and families (not all as verbal and emotional about it as Marie) who are nevertheless exercised in their souls over what Christmas has become, even in Christian circles. They are refusing to be dazzled out of their priorities at Christmastime.

The question arises, "How do I explain? I can't just stop giving Christmas gifts to relatives and friends."

It need not be a matter of stopping altogether; it can be a cutting down of the list and giving less pretentious items. To relatives and close friends, it may mean honestly spelling out your new convictions concerning Christmas extravagances and your intent to channel the money saved into contributions to the truly needy, in Christ's name.

I can hear someone say, "Oh, but that would sound so smug, so holier-than-thou. I don't want to have anyone think that about me."

All I can say to that point is, whenever Christians take a step of further commitment, there will be those who will not understand. When that step is directed by the Holy Spirit, to disobey is sin. We can risk being misunderstood, knowing that our giving in Jesus' name to the hungry and homeless is akin to presenting unto *Him* our gifts.

Activating that impulse

Bible Reading: John 14:16-17, 26;
1 Corinthians 14:10

Quench not the Spirit.
1 Thessalonians 5:19

"*I* just can't get that thought out of my mind."

How often have you been nagged by a persistent thought, an inner voice that refused to be stilled?

Paul, in his day, recognized the existence of many voices, "none of them without significance." Similarly, in our media-dominated society, so many voices clamor to be heard. This was reinforced for me a day or two ago as I stood in the checkout line of a supermarket. Said one shopper ahead of me, "I just don't know when to say yes en when to say no; there are so many demands —"

"You feel that way, too?" another woman broke in, in a resigned voice.

How should we proceed amid the tumult of voices that makes it all too easy to miss – or dismiss – the still small voice of God's Holy Spirit?

I distinctly recall such an instance when I could easily have failed God. After a busy day in my office I looked forward to an uninterrupted evening working on my own manuscript. But an impulse to call a particular friend kept intruding on my thoughts. I tried to push it away but without success. Admittedly, it was with some irritation I finally picked up my phone and called this friend. After a few rings I almost hung up, rationalizing, *There, I did my part*, when a weak voice that I scarcely recognized answered. "Oh, *Jeanette*," she said, "How did you know to call me tonight? I'm *so* sick – and I'm all alone."

I hastily left my unfinished chapter and drove the short distance to my friend's home. Along the way I thanked the Lord His Holy Spirit would not let me disregard His voice.

There's comfort for all of us in the assurance that God is always aware of our needs; He does hear the plea of His children, and one of His appointed means of answering our prayers is His nudging a fellow Christian into appropriate action – even though sometimes He has to insist and persist until we listen!

It may be that in order to more quickly recognize the

still small voice of God, we will have to consciously spend more time in His presence. We may even need to volunteer to be His hands or feet – or listening ears – to tell Him we are available; on call at any time. Think of the blessing (maybe adventures) that can lead to! Be an active partner with the Holy Spirit.

I just can't say no

Bible Reading: Luke 10:38-42

Mary hath chosen that good part, which shall not be taken away from her (v. 42).

"**How** did I get into this?" Ellen sighed as she contemplated her morning. "Why am I the one who gets snared into doing so much?"

Many women are victims of a can't-say-no mentality. These women are not necessarily smarter, more dependable, or blessed with more spare time than the rest of us. And, if they could bring themselves to admit it, they don't really want to always be saying yes.

Then how did Ellen's situation develop?

Generally, this type of person is quick to volunteer and has the ability to follow through with whatever she undertakes. It's gratifying for her to be recognized as being both willing and able; and gradually she finds herself swamped with things to do. Although it has been her own doing, she begins to feel resentful at other peoples's expectations.

It could be nursery duty in church, for instance. One may initially enjoy this duty but after a while may realize that along with the gratification is a sense of losing touch with other areas of church fellowship.

How much better not to allow this situation to develop in the first place. But how to avoid or prevent it? Why would an otherwise well-balanced, sensible person have difficulty in saying, "No, not this time; perhaps some other time"?

We all need to learn that at times no is a very good word.

"But," I hear someone protest, "I'm a *Christian!* Doesn't that mean I should always be willing to do my part?"

It's not for us to judge one another's dedication. But we do have the incomparable example in Mary and Martha. The Lord Jesus knew what the right priorities can do for us. While Martha was doing *good* things in being a hostess and caring for the household duties, Jesus saw beyond to a *better* thing that occupied Mary. And in order to spend time with the Lord, Mary had, no doubt, to say no to Martha for a time.

Sometimes we may need to say a firm no to ourselves. We can create our own bind by crowding our hours with things to do and places to go.

When we feel we must say no, we may still need to learn to stick to it, not be talked into changing our minds.

The first important step in learning to say no when appropriate is to remind ourselves that as children of God, we are valuable to Him and accountable to Him for how we spend our days. It's a biblical truth that we are not our own.

In the matter of our use of time, I've learned that saying no to some things frees me to say yes to more essential things.

A lesson in patience

Bible Reading: Romans 5:1-6

Let patience have her perfect work.
James 1:4

"**I** want patience – and I want it *now*" has become a cliché; but, if you are anything like me, there's a good measure of truth in this "want".

God is patient with us, however, and He teaches us if and when we let Him. I recall a common enough instance through which I learned a much-needed lesson. Three friends and I had arranged to meet for lunch at a particular time and place. Arriving first, I seated myself in a comfortable chair in the attractive lobby. Minutes went by: five – ten – fifteen, and I began to get decidedly impatient. *If I could be on time, why couldn't they? They'd better have a good explanation. After all, my time is valuable.* I became more irritated by the minute.

Before I could feel too superior, a voice whispered, "Right now you have a choice as to your words and actions."

Intrigued, I considered how I might greet my tardy friends. I could frown and say, "Wherever have you *been?* I've waited the longest time for you." Or, I could smile as I stepped forward to meet them, and say, "Here you are! What a good time we're going to have together." There was no need to question why anyone was late, which would have sparked a disturbing discussion and lessened the possibility of good time.

Not that I'm commending lateness as a habitual practice. There are people who have earned a name for that one thing: they can be counted on to be late. Their virtues tend to go unappreciated when habitual tardiness has branded them.

Why should any of us be patient with such people?

1. Because none of us is invariably punctual;
2. Because we can't always know the circumstances that have created the lateness;
3. Because we expect a measure of understanding and patience from our friends.

Moreover, the Bible exhorts us to let patience have her perfect work (James 1:4). We learn and grow as we let God work in our lives through otherwise frustrating situations.

"Patience is a virtue; virtue is a grace," we say, and who among us doesn't want to be graceful?

Measure for measure

Bible Reading: Matthew 6:9-15

And forgive us ... as we forgive (v. 12).

What does the Bible mean by "as" in the context of forgiving?

Clearly we are dealing with the laws of cause and effect: we do something or don't do it – and as a result something happens.

"As" can refer to the manner in which we "forgive". Some people say, "I forgive you," and you *feel* forgiven. By contrast, I heard a child say – and I wondered where the insight came from – "Auntie says she forgives me, but she really hasn't; I can tell." It could be that this child senses a "you don't deserve to have me forgive you" in her aunt's attitude.

Then there's the conditional "I'll forgive you if you

don't do it again." I overheard a young fellow say, in this instance, "It just makes me want to do the same thing again. Folks seem to think I can't be trusted to have learned my lesson when I admit I was wrong and ask their forgiveness."

Another "as we forgive" can be the holier-than-thou mouthing of the "I forgive you" while the expression denotes, "*I* would never do what you did."

Then there is the *extent* of forgiving, the measure of it, the totality. The Bible makes many references to the limitlessness of God's forgiveness – none more graphic than Psalm 103:12: "As far as the east is from the west, so far hath he removed our transgressions from us."

Have you ever tried to bridge the distance between East and West? Kipling stated both universal as well as poetic truth with his "East is east and west is west and never the twain shall meet" (from "Ballad of East and West").

Possibly the most significant meaning of "*as* you forgive" is the genuineness of it. The forgiven person is conscious of the other's sincerity. There's no hidden agenda, saying, "I forgive you," but figuratively filing the offense to bring it up at a later time.

We are not God. We can never approximate His power and willingness to forgive. Nevertheless, by His Spirit, we can become forgiving followers of our Lord, seeking to use His measuring cup as we mete out our forgiveness to others.

Me – a do-gooder

Bible Reading: Psalm 37:1-5

Trust in the Lord, and do good (v. 3).

The topic of the group Bible study was faith and works. During a discussion period, Alice said, "I wouldn't want to be called a 'do-gooder.'"

Why should this term *do-gooder* have such a negative connotation in a Christian's mind? Why can't "do good" mean just what it says?

This thought impressed me recently as I was reading Psalm 37. *How clear, how specific*, I realized. This was God Himself giving us two brief definite directives:

1. Trust Him.
2. Do good.

And the rewards for obeying are clearly spelled out –
practical rewards.

Most of us would strongly assert that we trust the Lord.
But honesty might make us admit we are less certain of
how much good we do in the world.

Trusting God is a state of heart and mind.

Doing good can be called a "state" of hands and feet,
a spirit of willingness to help other people. Combined,
better than anything else, they can demonstrate to an
unconvinced friend or neighbor that Christianity is
credible.

"What specific good can I do?" you may be asking.
That will depend on the kind of person you are, on the
needs around you, and on your abilities and willingness
to reach out and *do* something to help.

Some people have the gift of helps. These are natural
do-gooders. For others, myself among them, doing good
is not the first thing that comes to mind. Even so, we are
accountable to God for how we obey His directives.

Doing good involves time. There's no way we can
give of ourselves to help another without surrendering
some of our precious time. Yet there's rarely an occasion
when we cannot find time to be a helper. It may mean
giving up some pet project in order to be a good neighbor
to someone in need.

We say of some who seem to major in doing good, "I
wonder where they get the time?" That's no mystery.
We all have the same allotment of time: twenty-four

hours in a day. And one of God's intentions for us is that we use part of it in *doing good*. Our example? Our Lord Himself, of whom it is written, "Jesus ... went about doing good" (Acts 10:38).

The power of a smile

Bible Reading: Mark 10:13-16

A merry heart maketh a cheerful countenance.
Proverbs 15:13

In our relationships with people, some things are so simple that they may be overlooked. For instance, a *smile* is the finest medium of exchange we possess. A smile can dramatically change one's appearance for the better. If you doubt this, try standing in front of a mirror, wearing your "usual" face, and say, "This is what people generally see when they look at me." Then smile at yourself in the mirror. Now what would people see? A light in your eyes, the corners of your mouth turned up rather than grimly down? And – admit it – you *feel* better when you see the smiling you.

We live in a world where many people are harried and

frustrated and tired. Frown lines are carved into too many faces. But try smiling at them. It's important not to wait for the other person to smile first; she may be waiting for you!

A smile is the shortest distance between two people. When you smile, not only are you meeting someone's need for a spot of human warmth, but you are also meeting your own emotional needs as the other responds.

Some people claim that Jesus never smiled. They didn't get *that* out of the Bible! How can I be so sure? Because I know a little about children; I'm certain that, then or now, a child would shrink from an unsmiling, grim-visaged person. The very opposite is inherent in "He took them up in His arms."

How vital, then, that as Christian parents, Sunday school teachers, and others who influence the children around us, we reflect something of Jesus' warmth and concern for little children. At the very least, we can smile.

A smile cuts across all language barriers. After I had visited my daughter, a missionary nurse in what is now Bangladesh, I asked her, "Do any of your people remember me?" Her response: "What a question! Of course they do. They tell me, 'Your Mama smiled a lot.'" I couldn't speak a word of *Bengali*, but I could smile in their language!

Likewise, a smile recognizes no age limits. Watch a baby's face light up or an elderly person respond to a warm smile.

A smile, while costing us not a penny, is priceless for building relationships.

A smile is something you and I can afford to give – and be the richer for having given it.

If I only knew

Bible Reading: Exodus 33:11-18

*My presence shall go with thee,
and I will give thee rest. (v. 14).*

$\mathcal{M}$arcia and her friend Ellen were chatting on the phone, and when Marcia began to confide a particular problem, Ellen said, "Come on over and have a cup of tea, and we can talk." (I can certainly understand such a suggestion, for my Scottish mother's panacea for all ills was "a nice hot cup of tea.")

Over the tea together, Marcia sighed as she said, "If I just knew where it's all leading!"

This desire to know what lies ahead did not originate with our generation. Moses, in his day, petitioned God to "show him." Moses' request was twofold: knowledge of all that lay ahead of him, and a glimpse of God's glory. What if God had given Moses a preview of the future: the rebellious Israelites and the wilderness journeys that would try his soul? The sheer weight of the difficulties ahead might have caused him to give up on the spot.

And, had God given Moses a sight of His glory, might not Moses have been so blinded by the splendor that he immediately would have become homesick for heaven – useless for the task God had ordained for him?

Rather than grant His servant Moses' requests, our all-knowing God gave him the supreme assurance. *"My Presence shall go with you."*

Knowledge of the future, or the presence of God all the way: which would you rather have? Which would I rather have?

Let's consider what full knowledge of our future would do for us. Would it be likely to make us more wise, more able to contend with whatever came our way? Or would it keep us awake nights dreading morning's light, unfitting us for a new day with its known problems, snares, and pain?

I'm reminded of some lines of a hymn that begin, "If we could know as God doth know ..."

and end, "But God, in love, a veil has thrown across our way."

In His grace and mercy God has chosen to shield us from a full knowledge of what lies ahead.

In its place we have the comfort and assurance that

we will not walk alone. His presence will go with us, and He will give us rest – rest from fears, from doubts.

Why wouldn't we choose what proved sufficient for Moses? Has not our God granted us the light of His presence until this very hour?

Have a good night

Bible Reading: Psalms 4:8; 127:1-2

He giveth his beloved sleep (v. 2).

"Have a nice day!" Can you remember when you could hardly escape hearing that tired old phrase? (I was amused at a rebuttal poster that read, "Don't tell *me* what kind of a day to have.")

In the same vein we bid people good night. But common sense tells us that our words have no power in themselves to assure anyone of a good night, since surely the best of all good nights is the one during which we enjoy restful, restorative sleep.

That a lack of sleep on the part of otherwise normal, healthy people is widespread is attested to by the ever increasing panaceas on drugstore shelves and the volume of commercials for sleep aids.

Christians are not immune, which is understandable, considering that we are prone to the same pressures and stress as the world around us. But some believers have found the prescription – and it's free!

Sleep is a gift – a free gift – and only God can guarantee it will work. Meanwhile some of us depend on the world's solutions. On this subject, I heard a woman declare, "If I'm going to be dependent, *let me be dependent on God."*

What might reasonably contribute to habitual sleeplessness and thus the need for some sleep aid?

High on the list is worry or anxiety.

God's prescription? "Be anxious for nothing" (Philippians 4:6, NASB). Why should we not be anxious? Because God is not asleep; He is in control of our lives day and night if we will let Him be.

Another sleep deterrent is fear.

Certainly we're living in fearful days and nights when crime is no respecter of persons. Nevertheless, we have the scriptural injunction "Fear not." And have you pondered that freedom from fear was the first announcement to the shepherds at Christ's birth? "Tidings of great joy" followed, but first their fear was dispelled.

Guilt feelings prevent many Christians from enjoying a good night's sleep. God has His "cure" for this problem, also. "There is therefore now no condemnation to them which are in Christ Jesus" (Romans 8:1). If, before we seek sleep, we confess our sins and seek God's forgiveness, guilt can have no hold over us. All we have to do is believe God's Word.

Delivered from anxiety, fear, and guilt, we can relax in the peace that is ours and the assurance of a good night, for "He giveth His beloved sleep."

As an added tip, let me tell you what invariably helps me fall asleep: saying to myself some favorite Bible verses I've memorized, in particular Psalm 91. There will be particular verses that especially speak to you.

What's wrong with crying?

Bible Reading: John 11:30-35

Blessed are ye that weep now: for ye shall laugh.
Luke 6:21

$\mathcal{A}$t a church social function, a few of the members were discussing two recent deaths in their midst, and in particular the reaction of the new widows. Said one woman, "I just can't understand it. There's Sarah; she's taken her husband's death so well, but *Joan*" – she rolled her eyes – "you'd think she isn't even a *Christian*, the way she cries over her loss."

I have long realized that we sift each new happening in our lives through all our earlier experiences. This can explain why the one church member was "taking it so well," while the other (if people had ears to hear) was crying, "Help me! I can't get up."

Perhaps we all need to consider that there is nothing wrong with displaying our emotions. God gave us these emotions. Sometimes the Christian church appears to frown on any open expression of grief. But this would have to be contrary to the very nature of God as revealed in the Bible. Jesus displayed emotion. Jesus wept – He did not repress His tears at the grave of His friend Lazarus. Yet how often we, His followers, express admiration for the bereaved person who doesn't cry, who "bears up" under the trial.

When the film *The Hiding Place* was shown in my area, I overheard such admissions as, "I *cried* when I saw it"; "I almost cried"; "I had a time to keep from crying." Is it an achievement to keep from crying when tears would be a reasonable response? Is there something wrong with weeping when we're moved to tears?

A man of my acquaintance said to his wife, "You know if I go to [a certain place] I'll cry – and you wouldn't like that." I should explain that this man is no weakling, no sissy – far from it! And how did his wife respond? "Don't you know that this is one of the things I love you for – that you *can* cry?"

Sometimes we can learn eternally great lessons from a little child. Here's one. Janey came home from her playing with a little neighbor. "Mommy," she said, "Kathy was very sad because her puppy died." Then, her face brightening, she added, "But I helped her when she cried."

"Oh," said her mother, "that's good. Did you tell her not to cry anymore?"

"*No*, Mommy," Kathy corrected her. "I cried with her."

We can take comfort knowing that when tears overwhelm us, Jesus is there. He understands all about our griefs and our sorrows. As He cried with Martha and Mary, we can be sure He sympathizes with us. He will not reproach us for crying over the death of a loved one.

The fact is that there's nothing wrong with crying. And, having stood by them while they wept, we can likewise share in their rejoicing over new blessings, as Jesus promised (Luke 6:21).

Perfectionism: How desirable is it?

Bible Reading: Philippians 3:7-14

Whatever was to my profit I now consider loss for the sake of Christ (v. 7, NIV).

Speaking of her pastor's wife, Marilyn said – and a keen eye could have detected her admiration – "She's a *perfectionist*."

I admit to having had such aspirations for myself, until I learned better. Through a variety of experiences I've come to realize that the perfectionist is not generally a happy person. Always striving, driving herself, but never quite coming up to her own expectations of herself, she lives with frustration on many levels. It's devastating to her to realize she has made a mistake. "How *could* I?"

she berates herself (as though anyone can go through life without flubbing at one time or another).

The whole perfectionism concept is at odds with the Word of God. I have a feeling that the apostle Paul may have had to battle such a disposition. He certainly came to realize, as he wrote (v. 12), "Not as though ... I were already perfect ..."

Perfectionism can lead to loneliness, for, in addition to putting herself down, the perfectionist may demean other people who fall short of her unreal expectations of them; and friendship, which can't flourish in such an atmosphere, withers.

Sometimes children are the victims of even a loving mother when she is obsessed with "doing everything just right." For example, seven-year-old Mellisa offers to do the dishes. Pleased with her efforts at cleaning up the kitchen, she invites her mama to "come and see."

"What a good little girl you are!" her mother responds, then kills it with, "But why didn't you hang up the towel?"

Such a remark can only discourage even the most eager-to-help child. Not that I am by any means against coaching the child for better results; but there's a fine line between the desirable pursuit of excellence and the destructiveness of rigid perfectionism – which so often exhibits itself in criticism.

The much tossed around "nobody's perfect" is more than a cliché; it's biblical truth. We are imperfect people living in an imperfect world. This need not disillusion us, however. With our Lord's help we can go on, and, far from discouraging other pilgrims along the way by our insistence on perfection, we can be encouragers.

I'm pressing on the upward way;
New heights I'm gaining ev'ry day;
Still praying as I'm onward bound,
Lord, plant my feet on higher ground.
(Johnson Oatman, Jr.)

Can you afford it?

Bible Reading: Proverbs 16:20-24

He that handleth a matter wisely shall find good (v. 20).

$\mathcal{M}$argaret and a friend were just pulling into the driveway when a neighbor came out and got into her car.

Her eyes flashing, Margaret almost hissed, "I'd sure like to give that woman a piece of my mind."

"Are you sure you can afford it?" the friend responded jokingly.

The incident passed, but later, when she was alone, Margaret found herself dwelling on her friend's remark. Well might she – and those of us who call ourselves followers of the meek and lowly Jesus – consider whether *we* can afford to rail at a neighbor, however justified we may feel in doing so.

There's more than one good reason our "giving as good as we get" is no solution. We just might be left with a bitter taste in our mouths – from eating our own words!

Moreover, the Bible is quite explicit as to how we are to treat our neighbors: we are to love them, which is one of the two commandments our Lord taught and which is recorded in three gospels (Matthew 5:43-44; Mark 12:31; Luke 10:27) and in many other portions of the Bible.

There is great inner satisfaction in being loving rather than getting even. Lashing out at our neighbor is never God's will or God's way for us to relieve our feelings of anger or resentment. So can we afford to?

What we can afford is to emulate our Lord Jesus Christ, who, "when he was reviled, reviled not again" (1 Peter 2:23).

We can afford to use pleasant words. Although we can't be sure how our words will be received, neither are we responsible for the neighbor's attitude and/or response.

In my own experience, however, I've found that when I am willing to humble myself and go to someone with whom I have strained feelings (for whatever reason), the Lord has gone before, preparing both our hearts.

It will always be true, as Solomon wrote, "a soft answer turneth away wrath" (Proverbs 15:1).

Perhaps we need to add that "just forgetting" some unpleasant situation with a neighbor or friend is no way to cope with it. That would be like leaving a sore uncleansed, unattended. The result is that it festers. As believers in Jesus, we can apply words of love with all their healing power. And we *can* afford it.

The sustaining power of hope

Bible Reading: Psalm 146:1-6

Happy is he that hath the God of Jacob for his help, whose hope is in the Lord his God (v. 5).

*H*ow often have you seen someone throw up her hands and sigh as she said, "It's just *hopeless*. Everything is hopeless"?

I have to admit to being guilty at times of such faithless thinking.

Yet the Bible abounds in assurances that there is hope.

What generally contributes to our feelings of hopelessness? It can be ill health, a lack of something we need, the loss of someone we love, disappointment, or disillusionment – any number of things, because we are all different, and thus things affect us differently, which truth should make us tolerant of one another.

Many of God's servants have known the despair of hopelessness as well as the delights of hope. King David, for instance, came to the place of feeling so downcast that he even questioned why God had forsaken him (see Psalms 22, 42). But David realized the source of hope and answered his own soul's question with, "Hope thou in God" (Psalm 42:11).

"While there's life, there's hope" may be trite, but it is true. And this is no idle hope. It's logical. Think back to some situation that appeared totally hopeless. Then, given a little time (or perhaps even immediately), some circumstance arose to change the whole picture.

We can never separate hope and faith. A homey illustration comes to my mind: when my daughter Jeannie was a little girl, she had her own brand of faith and hope. More than once when we were planning a family picnic and the weatherman would dampen our hopes with his prediction of all-day showers, she would shrug and say, "Mommy, he doesn't know; he hasn't even asked *Jesus*." Then she would go about her own preparations for outdoor fun. Let me add that this well-balanced attitude of faith and hope has seen her through war, famine, cyclones, and other disasters as a missionary in Bangladesh.

Have you considered that in his "love chapter," 1 Corinthians 13, Paul includes *hope* in the top three virtues in the life of a believer? "And now abideth faith, hope, and love ..."

Whatever it is that may be causing you to feel hopeless today is not too much for God to handle.

"Hope to the end," Peter encourages us (1 Peter 1:3-9). It's not the end yet.

Why acceptance spells peace

Bible Reading: Philippians 4:5-13

I have learned ... to be content (v. 11).

$\mathcal{T}$he focus of the Tuesday Bible study was how we accept the will of God. "It's a great topic," Marian agreed, then added, "But I don't find it all that easy to practice."

Because it's a fact of life that no one – not even a child of God – escapes some trials, it is certainly worth thinking over how a Christian should act in the midst of them.

What are our options? We can resist and com-plain, or we can take it as from our loving heavenly Father and accept it. *There* is a sure formula for peace!

I'll never forget the day I stepped into a hospital room after a husband had asked if I would visit his wife who was dying. I didn't know her, but in a way she felt that she knew me. Weak as she was, she told me she had read a little booklet I had written titled *Acceptance Spells Peace** and that it had helped her deal with her feelings of resentment and anger against God and to trust Him to care for her husband and her children when she would no longer be with them. (May I interject here, for any reader who is also a writer, that these are the real rewards: the realization that God is pleased to use our words in the life of others who may need help in accepting His will and plan.)

When one's reaction to trouble is disbelief and resistance and a "poor me" attitude, we compound our problem, for we fracture our relationship with the Lord and are left to deal with it in our own strength and wisdom – or lack of it.

Built into our acceptance is our acknowledgment that God is working out *His* will and that, as a favorite few lines I've memorized state it,

> He knows; He loves; He cares;
> Nothing this truth can dim.
> God gives the very best to those
> Who leave the choice to Him.

And with this commitment of our way to Him, there's

a draining of resentment or rebellion against our circumstances. This concept is not only spiritual – many professionals in psychology and psychiatry acknowledge that indeed *acceptance spells peace*.

Why is peace the reward for acceptance?

God knows what is best for us, and it's no idle whim of His when He bids us, *"In everything give thanks"* (1 Thessalonians 5:18). It's a mystery to me how this can be the answer, but God does not have to explain Himself and His workings in our lives. Yet with multitudes in every age, one of the greatest discoveries is that a Christian can have genuine peace – soul and mind-calming peace – even while going through the problems that naturally would shatter us. The open secret? Acceptance.

Such an attitude may not prolong our lives, but it will most assuredly make them more serene.

Acceptance Spells Peace is available from the Narramore Christian Foundation, Box 5000, Rosemead, CA 91770.

The pluses of trouble

Bible Reading: Hebrews 12:6-11

My son, despise not thou the chastening of the Lord (v. 5).

$\mathcal{S}$peaking of a certain family in their church, Mary said to her friend Sandy, "The Lord must love them very much; nobody seems to have more trouble than they have."

"You have to be *kidding*," Sandy responded. "God wouldn't let His people go through one problem after another."

We can excuse Sandy for so thinking, for she's a new Christian. But many of us as more mature believers might have to admit to such a belief also.

Paul had no such illusions. He viewed trouble – and he certainly had his share – as something that *worked for him* (see 2 Corinthians 4:17) as a plus factor.

Whoever wrote the epistle to the Hebrews was of the same mind. We can imagine his saying, "Spare the rod and spoil the child" – in the interests of the child.

Acceptance of our heavenly Father's chastisement, learning from it, can only be for our own good, not to make God happy! And note the "afterwards." It may take patience to believe that good will come out of seeming "bad." But it will.

There's a condition attached to the promise of the good aftermath, the "peaceable fruit." This happy result is for those who are "exercised" by the problem: those whose faith is stretched and expanded, whose spiritual muscles are strengthened.

It helps to believe that God is not arbitrarily dispensing trouble, that He knows what is best for us. As Amy Carmichael wrote in her *Gold by Moonlight*, "God is completely trustworthy. All the deeper experiences of sorrow and comfort, temptation and victory, sooner or later turn out to be keys."

How insightful and true! Many of us can look back to experiences that tried our souls and tested our faith. Yet, when we have recognized the hand of God in the circumstances and trusted Him, we've seen Him use the trial as a key to open doors of opportunity of service for Him.

Such belief is the antidote to what Paul calls "a root of bitterness" (Hebrews 12:15) that might tempt us in times of trouble.

When, because we are human, we may be overwhelmed by trouble, we have the consolation of Psalm 46:1, *"God is ... a very present help in trouble,"* and, in the incomparable Psalm 91:15, *"I will be with him in trouble; I will deliver him."*

When trouble draws us nearer to God, then trouble is a plus.

Should I or shouldn't I?

Bible Reading: Psalm 25:1-5; Isaiah 30:21

Shew me thy ways, O Lord (v. 4).

"**I**'m so *indecisive*," Sarah admitted. "I just can't seem to make up my mind when I really need to."

Sarah is not alone. We all know people for whom decision-making is sheer trauma; it pulls them apart. It may be that as children they were never encouraged to choose; the choice was always made for them. This is not the best preparation for life.

For long enough I would have said that I knew how to make a good decision; I would even pass on my formula to anyone who asked me. I had four points:

1. Pray.
2. Set down in two columns the pros and cons.
3. Be objective.

4. If need be, counsel with someone in whom you
   have confidence.

Then I would add, "On the basis of all the facts, make
your decision – and live with it." (I had long heard that
a mark of maturity is one's ability to live with a decision.)

The only problem was – and I cringe as I think how
smugly I advised other people – I came to realize that
my formula *was not working for me!* Faced with a major
decision, I followed the process, but having decided, I
began to be plagued by a host of "what ifs."

I'll always remember the day I tossed the decision
question into the conversation hopper while at lunch
with some psychologist friends. Out of our discussion
came not some "shoulds," but the solid reasoning I had
been groping for.

If the decision is major, it has a time element involved.
Set a date, and make your decision on the basis of the
facts.

What was the key ingredient I had missed? Making
the decision on the basis of all you knew *at the time you
made it.* Be objective and honest with yourself – and it
will be a good decision *at the time.*

That was what I needed. Then one of my friends, Dr.
Ernest Shellinburg (whose help that day will always
stand out in my mind) added, "Subsequent happenings
may alter the facts, may even cause you to doubt the
wisdom of your decision; but at the time you made it, it

was a good decision."

Common sense then told me that I could vacillate the rest of my life while I waited for all the facts to come to light. Who do I think I am? I'm not God.

This may all seem like an oversimplification of the problem. To me, it came as comfort from God. I had been one who, coming to one of life's crossroads, would like to see just one sign pointing in one direction, preferably with my name on it.

God does give us direction; He does speak to us through His Word. Nevertheless, one of the glories of being His highest creation is that He lets us make our own decisions.

So pray for guidance, marshal the facts, use common sense, decide – and proceed from there. This is making a good decision.

A quiet time – what's that?

Bible Reading: Mark 1:32-35

He went ... apart to pray: and ... he was there alone.
Matthew 14:23

$\mathcal{A}$ few weeks after she had accepted Jesus as her Savior, Margaret asked one of her new friends, "What do you mean by 'quiet time'? I hear some of you talking about it. There's not much quiet time in our house, that's for sure."

We Christians are guilty of tossing around terms that have meaning only to us. Personally, I had no idea, as a new Christian, of some of the much-used Christianese. But I learned, and the importance of a time alone with God each day became significant to me.

When to have this set-apart appointment with the Lord is a problem for many Christians. I've always been inspired by the poem written by Ralph Spaulding Cushman, *The Secret*, in which the poet says he "met God in the morning when the day was at it's best."

In some religions, "meeting God in the morning" is mandatory. How often, in my travels in Muslim countries, I've been awakened before dawn by the plaintive Muslim call to prayer. Wherever the faithful are, or however sleepy they may be, they must obey this summons to pray.

I would hesitate to insist that first thing in the morning is the only or even the best time for everyone. However, I believe that we rob ourselves if we deliberately let something that can be done later interfere with this devotional time with our Lord. (He made it a priority when He dwelt among men.) And Satan will work overtime to keep us rationalizing, *I'll find time later on today*. I know about that. He has been all too successful at times in my own life, with less than happy consequences.

Like me, you may have to be reminded. I recall such an instance: I had listened to George Beverly Shea on the radio, singing "Fill My Cup, Lord." That lovely hymn haunted me, and I kept singing snatches of it. Suddenly it came to me just what I was asking God to do. Fill my cup – come and quench the thirsting of my soul – and I was not spending time alone with Him, not long enough for Him to even partially fill me (with Himself)! My "quiet time" was often more like reeling off a grocery list of requests than a plea for more of His Holy Spirit in my daily life.

What is a quiet time?

Just what we are willing to make it.

Help! I'm lost

Bible Reading: Psalm 32:7-11; 48:14

I will guide thee (v. 8).

"Coming to our brunch, Carolyn?" Mary asked, following the morning service. "We have a great group, and you'll enjoy the study, I'm sure."

"I'll be happy to come," Carolyn responded, "but how do I get there? You know me. I get lost."

Some people instinctively know their way around. Even in new surroundings they have no difficulty finding their way. Then there are the rest of us, sort of wandering souls who do not have that built-in radar, for whom getting lost is a lifelong frustration.

It's no fun feeling lost. I recall a rainy, chilly Saturday evening when I set out to attend a party to honor a colleague. In spite of the little map imprinted on the invitation, I got hopelessly lost. At one intersection, in sheer frustration I just *cried*. Then I said, "Lord, I don't know how to get there; and now *I don't know my way home!*" (Through the help of others, that evening was saved.)

Humiliating as it can be sometimes, I praise the Lord for lessons He keeps teaching me as I have to lean on Him.

"I will guide you," is God's promise. Some people give verbal directions; others offer a map (maps don't do a thing for me). The Lord says, in effect, "I know the way. I've been there. Let Me show you." And who wouldn't rather have a guide than a map!

There is nothing temporary about God's guidan-ce. He doesn't take us to a certain corner on life's journey then say, "There, you'll make it all right on your own now." No. His Word assures us, "For this God is our God for ever and ever: He will be our guide even unto death" (Psalm 48:14).

What about the spiritual ramifications of knowing that we are lost? What difference does it make? All the difference in time and eternity, for until we realize we are lost we will not be fit candidates for salvation. "For the Son of Man is come to seek and to save that which was lost" (Luke 19:10).

So there are benefits for the person who knows she is lost, who is willing to admit it and seek the help that is available.

What a comfort it is to realize that we don't have to worry about missing the way to heaven; we just have to follow Him who *is* the Way.

Love's dos and don'ts

Bible Reading: 1 Corinthians 13

Love is patient ... does not brag, is not arrogant.
v. 4, NASB

$\mathcal{F}$ive-year-old Jenny asked her mother, "Why are old people so grouchy?" (To Jenny, almost everybody was "old".)

The mother answered as best she could. The fact is, however, that no group – young, old, or in between – can be categorized as one thing or another. We are individuals with unique traits, whether good or not so good.

Notwithstanding, little Jenny's question is worth thinking about, whatever our age. For what we will be later, we are presently becoming. And we can't escape the fact that nobody is getting younger. Because of progress in knowledge of nutrition and health care, we can reasonably expect to live to be older than former generations. But each day we are around will be an added challenge to get along with other people.

Should you want to become crotchety – maybe even obnoxious – here are some ways to start:

Never listen to anyone else's views.
Expect the worst of everybody.
Demand your "rights".
Respect nobody's opinion but your own.
Keep your feelings sticking out so they can easily be hurt.
Remember every little injury anyone ever did you.

There are others, but these will do for starters. Fortunately, by contrast the Bible offers a total course in "How to Grow Older Gracefully." This short course is complete in what has come to be known as the "love chapter," 1 Corinthians 13. Let's look at verses 4-8a (NIV).

Love is patient, love is kind. It does not envy, it does not boast, it is not proud. It is not rude, it is not self-seeking, it is not easily angered, it keeps no record of wrongs. Love does not delight in evil but rejoices with the truth. It always protects, always trusts, always hopes, always perseveres. Love never fails.

The encouraging thing about God's "how-tos" is that He doesn't leave us with just His manual of instruction. With it, by His Spirit He gives us the enabling to make it work in our individual lives. If we really want to be loving Christians, showing forth to those around us what a loving God is really like, we can be sure it will not have to be a do-it-ourselves pursuit. He will be with us as we seek to exemplify the love chapter in our everyday lives.

Combating the monotony

Bible Reading: Psalm 92:12-15

They shall still bring forth fruit in old age (v. 14).

Jane is no whiner. But one day as I visited her in an attractive residence for seniors, she revealed her chief dissatisfaction with her new way of life. "It's the sameness, the *awful sameness*," she said sadly.

Here is a woman who all her life had been actively engaged in useful pursuits and for whom books were her daily delight. Now, her sight deteriorating, she is deprived of much reading as well as the handicrafts at which she excelled. Even her walks, with their discoveries along the way, are curtailed. With almost no variety in her day, the predictability of it all was getting to her spirit.

There's no pat solution to Jane's problem, and she is

by no means alone in her circumstances. Age naturally brings with it a diminishing of one's faculties, and many people have difficulty in adjusting to a less desirable way of life.

One person can encourage another, however, in the knowledge that God has new experiences for us each day if we will but look for them. Both His compassion and His mercies are "new every morning," as we read in Lamentations 3:22-23 (the portion of Scripture from which we get the inspiring hymn "Great Is Thy Faithfulness").

Can there, I wonder, be a better panacea for the deadly sameness of one's days than to know that He abideth faithful? We all like new things: new clothes, new kinds of food, new experiences, making new friends. The world is filled with new things – and God is adding to them each morning.

Not all that is new is necessarily desirable. Perhaps that is why as we grow older we want to hang on to the familiar. There's nothing wrong about having a wish that all things might remain as they have been. But it's not natural that they should. Our God is the author of variety in every form of life: we see it all around us, and change is a part of it.

The glorious truth that sustains us, wherever we are and whatever our external circumstance, is that God is always with us: He never changes. He has said, "I am the Lord, I change not" (Malachi 3:6).

When Jane, and others in like circumstances, can comprehend that God still has a plan for their lives – that they are a part of *His* plan – the boredom, the sameness can give place to a new excitement with their present lives.

Win the argument – lose a friend

Bible Reading: Proverbs 15:1-7

A wholesome tongue is a tree of life; but perverseness therein is a breach in the spirit (v. 4).

"*L*et's sit at that other table," Ruth suggested, steering her friend away from where she was about to be seated.

"Why did you want to be here, particularly?" Sara asked. "What was wrong with where I was?"

"It's not the table, Sara. It's who's at it. I just don't feel like getting into some argument with Dorothy. She just has to argue over every little thing."

Do you know people like that? Or maybe the question should be, Are *you* like Dorothy? Dorothy couldn't keep a friend, and she couldn't figure out why. She liked people, was outgoing, and was always willing to pull her weight when there was a job to do. People who at first welcomed her and included her in their doings would after a short time shed her as they would a second skin they could do without.

It was not until another woman was caring enough to broach the subject that Dorothy began to wake up to what her problem really was. They talked a bit, then Dorothy said in amazement, "Am I hearing you say that I always have to have the last word?"

"Not only that," the friend explained, "*you always have to be right*. That alienates people."

There's one in every group, or so it seems. They will argue and argue, generally about something that doesn't matter and that nobody can do anything about. I have heard such people battle over whether it rained last Tuesday or about which day they had fish for dinner.

Now if there are two people and one insists "I am *right*," what does it do for the other person? It's certainly no way to make or keep a friend. In fact, there is scarcely a surer way to fracture a friendship.

There has to be a great sense of insecurity in the "always right" individuals who use this tactic as an ego builder. But it backfires. Knowingly or unknowingly, they are what the Bible calls wise in their own conceit; they lean on their own understanding, which is always a dangerous way to go.

Have you thought that our Lord could have asserted

under every circumstance, *"I am right"?* It would have been true. Jesus would not stoop to such a put-down practice, for it never fails to leave the other person feeling resentful and angry. (There is a time to insist that we're right: when truth and values are at stake. But that's another subject.)

Sadly, it's the phraseology that hurts. There's nothing remiss in pointing out – kindly – that something is not accurate. It's the accusing "you" that we react to; the *"you* are wrong" that is always inherent in *"I* am right."

We can choose to be "right" every time and go our lonely way, or we can acknowledge this negative trait and ask God to help us overcome it.

Somebody has to tell them

Bible Reading: Psalm 78:1-8

*Declare them to their children, that they
might set their hope in God (vv. 6-7).*

Who is making God real to today's children?

You may feel a desire to be the one to share the truth of God's love with them. "But," you rationalize, "today's children are such sophisticated little people; they have so much, and they seem to know so much."

True. Even some of their toys are beyond our understanding. Nevertheless, have you ever known a child who didn't like stories? Not long ago I listened in on a conversation between two adorable four year olds who were trying one-upmanship on each other: "My grandma buys me the nicest toys – and candy, too," bragged Susie.

"Oh, but *my* grandma *tells me stories* and *she reads to*

me," countered Lory in a you-can-keep-your-old-toys tone.

What were these little girls expressing? One was saying that her grandmother spent money on her; the other was speaking of a grandmother who spent time with her.

It does take time to sit down and tell or read a story (and one is never enough, and anyone who does well knows!). But how rewarding the result can be!

We don't all have *Little House on the Prairie* tales to recount, but we do have experiences to relate. And we have the *Bible*.

Some years ago I visited a little relative who was sick. There was a Bible in her room, although at that time her parents were not yet believers in Christ. She asked me to tell her a story, and my mind went to the child Samuel whom God had talked to. So I reached for the Bible and read from 1 Samuel 3. Janice was fascinated, and a day or so later her mother called and asked, "Where can I find in the Bible a story about God talking to a little boy *by name?*" She sounded exasperated as she explained, "Janice is bugging me to read it to her – and I can't find it."

We never can tell which Bible truth children's minds will latch on to. We never know the effect it will have on them for life. But we can feed into them our own assurance, from experience, of a God who is so interested in every child that He knows each by name as He knew

Samuel.

By not hiding from children these things that praise and honor God (Psalm 78:4), we can start a chain reaction that results in future generations knowing God and making Him known to *their* children.

Somebody has to ignite the spark. What a privilege to be that one!

Being a gracious taker

Bible Reading: Psalm 116:1-4, 12-13

What shall I render unto the Lord for
all his benefits toward me? (v. 12).

$\mathcal{T}$he church had invited to their monthly congregational dinner some neighborhood families who were in poor economic circumstances. Discussing the success of this venture, the women's committee responsible for the dinner commented, "They [the visitors] just clung together, wouldn't mingle with our people, even though we did our best to encourage them to."

Listening to the church women's expressions of wonder, disappointment, and – yes – hurt at what some of them construed as "sheer ingratitude," one person said, "It's not all that easy to be the *taker*." An insightful remark, and how true!

We know that the Bible tells us it's more blessed to give than to receive. It is also more *easy*. Yet many of us can be blind to our own unease at having to be the recipient, especially of "charity."

This feeling comes into play in other settings, also. How well I remember the occasion when my eyes were opened to my own feelings. I had invited four friends to join my daughter and me for dinner at a favorite restaurant. When the waiter brought the check, not one but two of the others reached for it. Insisting that they were my guests, I almost made a scene over who should pay. Later, when we were alone, my daughter, Jeannie (after the preamble, "I want to say something to you, Mother; I think you can take it"), gave me this incomparable piece of advice: "You are very good at giving, but I think you need to learn to *take* things graciously."

I'm thankful that I listened and thought through what she was conveying to me. The word *graciously* spoke to me. Even as there are ways to give graciously, there are likewise gracious ways of taking.

David the psalmist had the right slant on this matter of give-and-take: recognizing all that the Lord God had done for Him, David was not at his wits' end for a way to reciprocate. To his own question, "What shall I give to the Lord for all his mercies to me?" he answered, "I will *take* the cup of salvation" (emphasis added).

Actually we are all needy creatures dependent on other

people, perhaps more than we care to admit. Certainly there is one vital need we can never meet on our own. *We can't save our own souls*. Even the great king of Israel could not do that. He proves his willingness to be a taker in this greatest of all acceptances: "I will take the cup of salvation."

As we, individually, take God's offer of salvation through Jesus Christ and He becomes Lord of our lives, we can begin to give out to others the good news.

It *is* possible to be both a gracious giver and a gracious taker.

Let's talk about Jesus

Bible Reading: Luke 24:13-18

Jesus himself drew near (v. 15).

Susan was just a little girl when her much-loved grandfather listened to the message of the gospel and became a believer. Almost immediately his new faith was reflected in his violin playing around the home. His favorite chorus was the then popular "Let's Talk About Jesus." When Susan heard someone else singing this piece, she was quick to exclaim, "That's my *grandpa's* song!"

It would be worth considering how we, by what we sing or by our conversation, impress those with whom we come in contact.

It was as the two followers of Christ were talking of Him so earnestly that Jesus Himself appeared and joined them. Not many of us will walk that Emmaus road; but we don't need to in order to have our Lord Himself present with us. He has said, "Where two or three are gathered together in my name, there am I in the midst of them" (Matthew 18:20). Surely when we've met in His name, we will be talking about *Him* – or are we talking about everyone and everything else?

A verse I might never have discovered for myself is Malachi 3:16. As a new Christian in a church where the members regularly stood and gave testimony to their faith in Jesus, I heard one person invariably quote this verse: "Then those who feared the Lord talked with each other, and the Lord listened and heard" (NIV). In a sense those believers said to each other, "Let's talk about the Lord."

We might do a profitable study of what happens and *doesn't* happen when we focus our conversation on our Lord and what pleases Him when we get together.

For one thing, we will be a blessing to each other as we recount what God is doing in our lives (I still remember how those testimonies in my early Christian days encouraged me, making my new faith credible and practical). We will also pray intelligently for one another's needs. These are just a few of the benefits of "talking about Jesus."

Conversely, in this climate filled with Christ's presence (for He did promise to be with us), we will hesitate to gossip, to gripe, or to spend our time in fruitless, negative chatter. Our coming together as fellow Christians conscious that Jesus cares enough to be there with us will then be a positive, up-building experience. Let's do talk about Jesus!

The Susan in this story is my dear niece; her grandpa, my father.

The therapy of singing

Bible Reading: Ephesians 5:19-20

Singing and making melody in
your heart to the Lord (v. 19).

"**W**ant to stay younger looking?" the radio announcer
began, "Then join the church choir. Women who sing
exercise their facial muscles – thus preventing wrinkles."

As I listened, I thought, *That's not a very noble motive
for singing in the choir!* Anyway, what's so bad about a
few wrinkles? Are we ashamed of the years the Lord
has given us?

But we do have a good reason for singing. We sing
because, as the psalmist wrote, the Lord has put a song
in our hearts. We may not all be prospects for the church
choir, but that need not prevent us from singing to
ourselves, from making melody in our hearts unto the

111

Lord. He isn't checking out the quality of our performance.

From earliest record, music has been a part of human experience. Who originally taught music? Where did Jubal study organ and harp (see Genesis 4:21)? The first recorded lyrics? – Moses' song of victory, of redemption (Exodus 15). As New Testament believers, who has more to sing about than we do?

Apart from being an avenue of praise to God, singing has other benefits. It gives us an outlet to express our inner feelings. Singing can also affect our spirits.

Can you remain angry with someone while you're singing, "Jesus, Jesus, Jesus; there's just something about that name?" or, "Love divine, all loves excelling"? Can you dwell on how lonely you feel as you sing to yourself, *"I never walk alone, Christ walks beside me"*?

We rob ourselves when we never sing; a mother robs her children if they never hear her singing or humming about her work. I can never be thankful enough for my mother, who sang beautiful hymns that have stayed with me.

Sadly, some people have no one to sing to. But that need not stop them. In fact, it's a good reason for singing. Recently, a woman who heard me speak on this subject told me she lived alone.

"For days at a time," she explained, "I have no one to talk to, and sometimes I feel that I'm losing my voice from lack of using it. And I don't want to start talking to myself!"

"Why not try singing?" I suggested. "Sing along with a radio program or record. Or just *sing*. "Then I told her that I do this all the time when I'm driving alone. I sing and praise the Lord and feel blessed and inspired.

A crowning reason for singing here and now is that we can be tuning up to join the heavenly choir.

This just isn't my day

Bible Reading: Psalm 107:1-8

This is the day which the Lord hath made.
Psalm 118:24

*R*eaching for a piece of Danish, Elva tipped her cup, spilling a little coffee on her dress.

"It's just not my day," she said ruefully.

Tune in on another conversation, and we might hear, "In *my* day –"

In still another vein – a more positive one – Nancy glows as she tells about a piece of good fortune that's come her way and adds, "This must be my day."

Not to make light of the person's feelings or her reason(s) for making any of these "my day" statements, let's consider the possible ramifications of the phrases we use. Is there not some subtle implication in each that

114

some days are ours – those in which for one reason or another we feel gratified, feel good about ourselves and how things are going for us?

What about the other days? Whose days are they?

The psalmist had it right when he wrote, *"This is the day which the Lord hath made,"* and David knew what to do with the day.

I'm reminded of a dear friend, Ruth, whose husband, a strong, vital man, died suddenly, leaving her with two young daughters to raise without their beloved daddy.

I was her pastor's wife, and while her girls were in school we spent long hours together, drinking innumerable cups of tea as she spilled out the hurts, the fears for the future that beset her, and we prayed together. One day she said to me, "You know, when Pastor Lockerbie stands up in the pulpit and announces, 'This is the day the Lord has made; we will be glad and rejoice in it,' somehow everything seems all right; it makes me feel I can go on, that life *is* possible."

Have you noted the two little words *in it?* The psalmist emphasizes the immediacy of his rejoicing. Not rejoicing in and being glad by looking forward to "this day," and not by looking back on it. No. It's in the living of each day for itself.

"But how can I rejoice and be glad?" I hear someone say. "If you only knew –"

We can't always know what another is going through that makes it difficult for her to rejoice. Nor can we be judgmental about such things.

Nevertheless, not being Pollyannas but *because God is who He says He is*, we can rejoice and be glad in each day He graciously gives us. As Annie Johnson Flint writes in her poem:

> One day at a time,
> And the day is His day.

Majoring on the negatives?

Bible Reading: Luke 7:36-50

If our gospel be hid, it is hid to them that are lost.
2 Corinthians 4:3

The Browns had just moved to a new town, and ten-year-old Jerry was eager to find some boys of his own age to play with. Meanwhile his parents were equally interested that he make friends among Christians. Naturally they were delighted when Jerry came home all excited, telling them about his new friend Greg.

"And know what, Mom?" he added. "Greg goes to church and Sunday school and all. Isn't that great?"

Jerry's enthusiasm soon waned, however. Within the week he came home disconsolate, not even mentioning

Greg.

"What's the matter, son?" his dad asked. "You're awfully quiet these days. Sure you're feeling all right?"

"It's not that, Dad," Jerry answered. "It's, oh, I don't know. But Greg's not like us, I guess. His folks won't let him do things. He says Christians don't –" and the boy reeled off a number of restrictions that to him were puzzling. "I like Greg," he continued, "But I wouldn't want to be that kind of a Christian, would you, Dad? They must think that Jesus never wants us to have any fun!"

Whatever we might think of Greg's family, we can reasonably assume that they were not winning their neighborhood to Christ. People in general are not impressed by what we *don't* do.

With all the positives we as God's people have going for us, why should we major on the negatives?

With so much that needs to be done in so many realms to help and bless those around us, why be known only for pulling our skirts around us lest we become contaminated?

Our Lord is Himself our example, freely moving among the publicans and sinners, even though He was maligned for doing so. He knew what His mission was. He had come, He said, "to seek and to save that which was lost" (Luke 19:10).

It goes without saying that as Christians we do have our standards of behaviour. It's likewise true that we will at times be scoffed at for the beliefs that color our actions. And we do need to rear our children in the light of our Bible standards, trusting that when they themselves accept the Lord, they likewise will adhere to Christian principles.

Nevertheless, we need to habitually shy away from the nonbelievers among our neighbors. There are always a number of wholesome activities in which we, individually or as a family, can conscientiously participate with our unsaved friends and neighbors. Each one can provide a witnessing opportunity.

A verse that should prevent us from being Christian recluses, which has often spoken to me, is 2 Corinthians 4:3, "If our gospel be hid, it is hid to them that are lost."

The opposite verse? "Let your light so shine ..." (Matthew 5:16).

Comfort in the shadows

Bible Reading: Psalm 23

Thou art with me (v. 4).

*I*t was Kathleen's first appearance following the death of a family member. Sensitive to her feelings, her friends at the missionary luncheon guided their conversation toward comforting her, letting her talk out what was on her heart, and *listening* to her.

At one point Kathleen shared with them some-thing that had consoled her during her severe trial: "It was when Pastor talked with me about 'the valley of the shadow of death.' I had never really given any thought to that, although I've been able to quote the Twenty-third Psalm since I was a child."

Many of us can readily recite from memory the beloved "Shepherd Psalm." And it may be that, like Kathleen, we have not paused long enough at the fourth verse with its "shadow of death."

How can we – do we – when the occasion arises, comfort a bereaved person? Only as we ourselves know the comfort God gives through His Word.

The valley of the shadow of death: a dark valley, but our Lord passed through that valley. He took the sting out of death; He took the fear out of the darkness.

Our Lord defeated the substance, the last enemy, *death*. Now all that remains, for the believer in Jesus, are the shadows.

There never was or could be a shadow without the sunshine.

Not only did our Lord rob the valley of its shadows, but we are assured that He will also walk with His own through the valley. I love the lines of an old hymn:

> Jesus will walk with me
> Down through the valley;
> Jesus will walk with me
> All the way Home.

David realized this truth when he wrote confidently, "I will fear no evil: for thou art with me." The One who made the path now walks its length with the home-going child of God.

Why, then, should we fear the valley of the shadow of death?

Restocking the shelves of life

Bible Reading: Galatians 5:19-26

O Lord, thou hast searched me and known me.
Psalm 139:1

Joyce and Doris met for a quick cup of tea in the local mall before battling the crowds at the inventory sales. Rather thoughtfully, Doris remarked, "There must be some profit in all this hassle, or I'm sure the stores wouldn't bother to stage such sales."

"You're right," Joyce agreed, then added, "Maybe there's a lesson in it for us."

We might all profitably ask why businesses make such a production of their year-end inventory. To be sure, it's not just to give shoppers a chance to paw through the high-piled merchandise. They have a dual purpose in these sales extravaganzas: one, to scrap the no-longer-profitable merchandise; two, to restock with proven moneymakers and make room for new items.

As Joyce intimated, we can all learn from this practice.

In particular, what are some items or areas of life we can profitably discard? Undoubtedly, these will vary. We will have to be discriminating, taking as our criteria what applies to each one of us in today's reading. Nor can we smugly assert, "I'm not guilty of these vile things Paul exposed: I'm no murderer or idolator." But, before we pass on too hurriedly, let's be honest about the *hatred, wrath, variance, strife* that can hinder even the devout believers among us from being what God wants us to be. Having acknowledged these evils in our lives and sought the help of the ever-willing Holy Spirit in ridding us of them (as we walk in the Spirit), we can then proceed to restock the shelves of our lives.

And what a store we have to choose from! The whole line is there for us in verses 22-23: love, joy, peace, longsuffering, gentleness, goodness, faith, meekness, temperance. Take just the first three. How we could change our world if we would earnestly work at cultivating these fruits of the Spirit! I think my favorite is *joy*, for we are all projecting some kind of image as avowed Christians. The world needs joy-filled people in our often gloomy circumstances.

There's no need to wait until year's end to do our stocktaking and restocking. I know of a woman who follows this practice:

> Every night I recap my day,
> ask, "What did I do wrong today?
> How can I undo the wrong and learn
> from the experience? How can I help
> change things to make them better for
> other people as well as myself?"

Oh, I should tell you that this woman is a wheelchair-bound victim of arthritis.

You and I can find our own best way to reduce our less desirable qualities and then restock from the treasures God has for us in His Word. Happy inventory!

Restocking the shelves of life

Bible Reading: Galatians 5:19-26

O Lord, thou hast searched me and known me.
Psalm 139:1

Joyce and Doris met for a quick cup of tea in the local mall before battling the crowds at the inventory sales. Rather thoughtfully, Doris remarked, "There must be some profit in all this hassle, or I'm sure the stores wouldn't bother to stage such sales."

"You're right," Joyce agreed, then added, "Maybe there's a lesson in it for us."

We might all profitably ask why businesses make such a production of their year-end inventory. To be sure, it's not just to give shoppers a chance to paw through the high-piled merchandise. They have a dual purpose in these sales extravaganzas: one, to scrap the no-longer-profitable merchandise; two, to restock with proven moneymakers and make room for new items.

As Joyce intimated, we can all learn from this practice.

In particular, what are some items or areas of life we can profitably discard? Undoubtedly, these will vary. We will have to be discriminating, taking as our criteria what applies to each one of us in today's reading. Nor can we smugly assert, "I'm not guilty of these vile things Paul exposed: I'm no murderer or idolator." But, before we pass on too hurriedly, let's be honest about the *hatred, wrath, variance, strife* that can hinder even the devout believers among us from being what God wants us to be. Having acknowledged these evils in our lives and sought the help of the ever-willing Holy Spirit in ridding us of them (as we walk in the Spirit), we can then proceed to restock the shelves of our lives.

And what a store we have to choose from! The whole line is there for us in verses 22-23: love, joy, peace, longsuffering, gentleness, goodness, faith, meekness, temperance. Take just the first three. How we could change our world if we would earnestly work at cultivating these fruits of the Spirit! I think my favorite is *joy*, for we are all projecting some kind of image as avowed Christians. The world needs joy-filled people in our often gloomy circumstances.

There's no need to wait until year's end to do our stocktaking and restocking. I know of a woman who follows this practice:

> Every night I recap my day,
> ask, "What did I do wrong today?
> How can I undo the wrong and learn
> from the experience? How can I help
> change things to make them better for
> other people as well as myself?"

Oh, I should tell you that this woman is a wheelchair-bound victim of arthritis.

You and I can find our own best way to reduce our less desirable qualities and then restock from the treasures God has for us in His Word. Happy inventory!